A little Royal Black History

AUTHOR: TASHEEMA MARTIN

THIS BOOK IS DEDICATED TO

THE LITTLE KINGS AND QUEENS WHO INSPIRE ME.

This Book Belongs To

_____

This is the story of your ancestors;
the real history indeed.

You come from a grand backstory;
one of real kings and queens.

You may only know of slave history,
which is often taught in school.

And unfortunately, those stories
are filled with bondage and gloom.

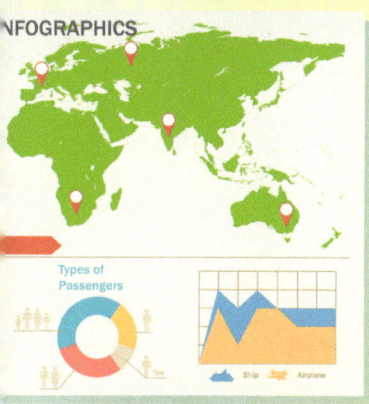

However, no worries about the erased stories and significant events taken.

There is no way that thousands of years of greatness could be stuffed within a few textbook pages.

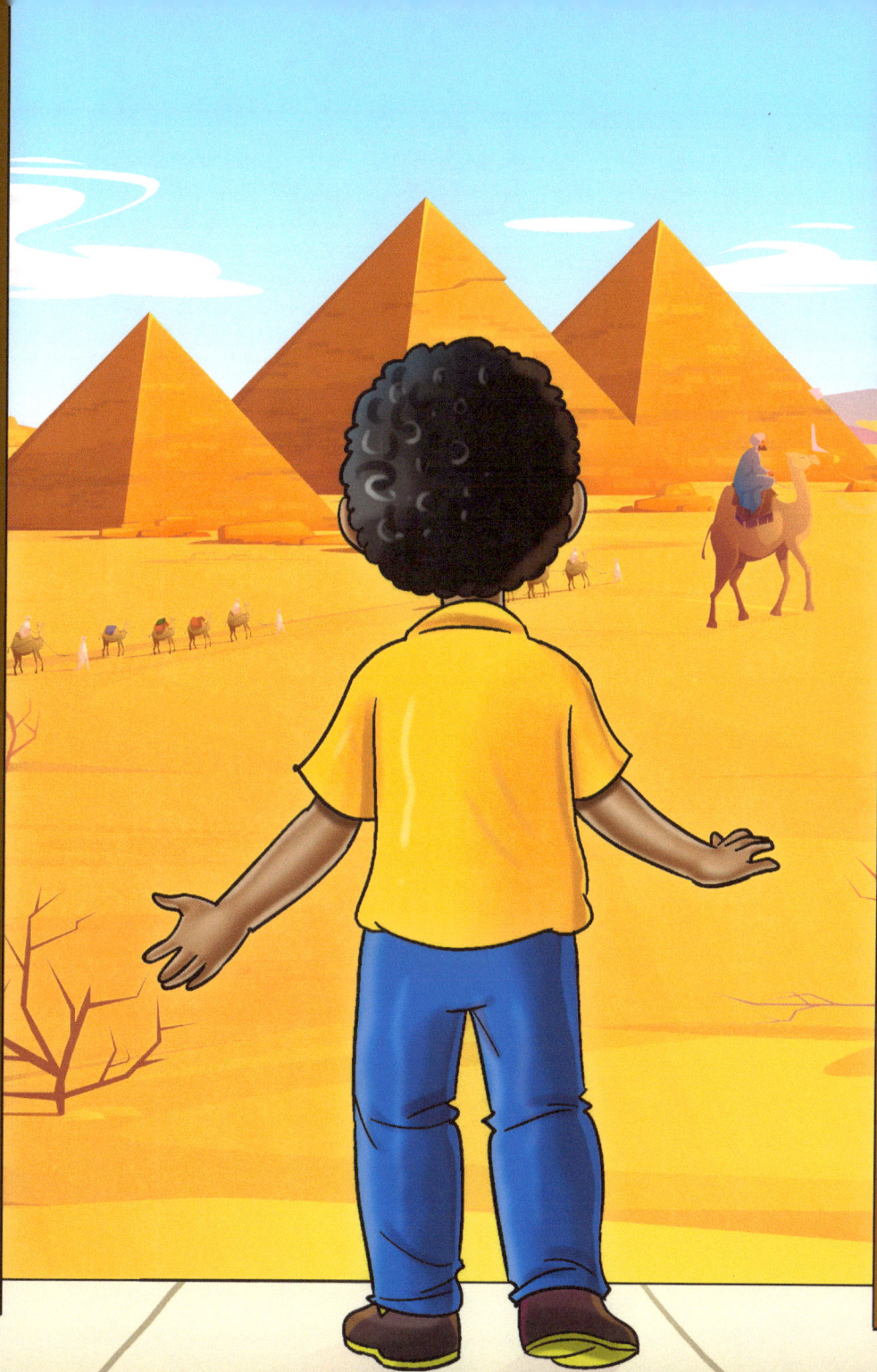

Ancient Egypt is what we know it as,
but "Kemet" is the native name.

Once again, this is something
that changed when the outsiders came.

Let's start with the great Nile River and along it lived an extraordinary group of people,

who settled on rich lands with gold and let's not forget about the temples.

They are responsible for
the greatest statues, elaborate tombs,
and pyramids that touch the sky.

These structures are known very well
around the world and highlight
their architectural side.

The people of Ancient Egypt were the first of many.

They were the first chemists, scientists, physicians, and phenomenal mathematicians.

Ancient Egypt influenced the art, music, and cosmetic industries as we know them today.

And overall are instrumental in creating and furthering civilization in a major way.

As you continue
learning about black history,
understand that it's a history
not only based on slavery but nobility.

And carrying those teachings
is now your responsibility.

So adjust your crowns boys and girls because you represent true royalty.

And knowing that you are the descendants of a culture that inspired everything around you, you can smile joyfully.

Author's Note

The purpose of writing *A Little Royal Black History* was to share a different narrative with our youth. I wanted to create a story that acknowledges and highlights the truly innovative and royal background that we come from, that inspired the world we live in today.

www.ingramcontent.com/pod-product-compliance
Lightning Source LLC
Chambersburg PA
CBHW042119040426
42449CB00002B/101